Meditation – The Vehicle to Stress Free and Creative Living

15 Ways to Benefit from the Mind's Higher Levels of Consciousness Connections

Power up your brain with meditation, a proven practice with thousands of scientific studies confirming what the ancients knew over six thousand years ago. Meditation is not a religion; it is a spiritual practice as we connect the body, mind, soul and spirit with all of creation. Meditation can:

- Increase brain tissue volume, enabling you to make better life choices
- Increase telomerase activity, which lengthens your life
- Promote inner calm and physical well-being

If you want to learn more about meditation, pick up this exciting and informative Itty Bitty® Book today.

Your Amazing Itty Bitty® Meditation Book

15 Ways to Benefit from the Mind's Consciousness Connections

Rhona Jordan,
C.GIt., C.CHt.

Published by Itty Bitty® Publishing
A subsidiary of S & P Productions, Inc.

Copyright © 2017 **Rhona Jordan, C.GIt., C.CHt.**

All rights reserved. No part of this book may be reproduced or transmitted in any form or by any means, electronic or mechanical, including photocopying, recording or by any information storage and retrieval system, without written permission of the publisher, except for inclusion of brief quotations in a review.

Printed in the United States of America

Itty Bitty® Publishing
311 Main Street, Suite D
El Segundo, CA 90245
(310) 640-8885

ISBN: 978-0-9992211-3-6

Photograph of Rhona Jordan courtesy of Paige Zak

Dedication

Sue Okuda-Stewart

Sue and I were enrolled in the Primordial Sound Meditation Instructor's course. We were study partners, and Sue was my rock when I did not think I could pass the intense study program exams. Sue and I are now Global Instructors for Deepak Chopra and the Chopra Center. Sue's encouragement and true understanding of the Vedic teachings pulled me through. Sue, on all levels, I am grateful for your friendship, knowledge and patience. Thank you.

Stop by our Itty Bitty® website to find interesting information regarding the practice of meditation in your daily life.

www.IttyBittyPublishing.com

Or visit Rhona Jordan at

www.rhonaimagery.com

Table of Contents

Introduction
Connection 1.   Synchronies
Connection 2.   The Science of Meditation
Connection 3.   OM Symbol
Connection 4.   Chanting OM
Connection 5.   OM and Earth's Rotation
Connection 6.   Mantra, Sound, Energy, Frequency, Vibration
Connection 7.   Primordial Sound Meditation Mantra
Connection 8.   How to Meditate
Connection 9.   Chakras
Connection 10.   The Lotus Flower
Connection 11.   Breathing
Connection 12.   Mala Beads
Connection 13.   Labyrinths
Connection 14.   Questions & Answers
Connection 15.   More Questions & Answers

Introduction

Research in the Journal of Neuroscience and the Journal of Stress Management stated that meditation reduced stress levels and pain intensity by 75%.

Meditation originated in India, but is considered universal, just like the discovery of electricity in the United States is considered universal. The six thousand-year history of meditation is based on the Vedic traditions in India, which teach that the universe within you is as vast as the cosmos surrounding you. Meditation is a portal to explore the gap between thoughts, a place of pure peace.

The word "yoga" means the union of the environment, senses, body, mind and soul. The yoga of meditation is not about forcing the mind to be quiet with no thoughts; it is about finding that silence between thoughts that is already there. That pause, space, gap, portal or quiet-centered awareness is the mind's connection to the source of creation.

A normal day is a series of three states of consciousness: awake, deep sleep, dreaming. In meditation, you transcend these first three states of consciousness. When we add meditation to the daily routine, we can enter into the 4th State of Consciousness, that of Transcendental Consciousness.

Meditation is not a religion; however, it is a spiritual practice as we connect the body, mind, soul, spirit and everything in creation together.

It is easy to overlook meditation's potential when you are in survival mode: paying bills, working, raising a family, responsibilities of all kinds. However, meditation changes our physical and emotional reaction to daily stress. Peace and calm replace survival mode, which in turn, becomes thrive mode.

- Meditation is used as a tool for rediscovering the body's own inner intelligence.
- Meditation is silent intelligence.
- Meditation is the most powerful and direct means to connect with the mind's deeper levels.
- Meditation activates a hidden universal force.
- Meditation empowers the mind to move the molecules in your body.

Consciousness Connection 1
Synchronies
Cosmic Inspiration

Synchronies are events that occur simultaneously, which we believe have meaning beyond mere coincidence. Whenever we make a conscious choice to experience something new or different, there is an inner call to take action. These are the synchronies leading to the writing of this book:

1. I attended a 7-day "Silent Awakening" event taught by Dr. Deepak Chopra.
2. 130 participants attended and maintained total silence as we followed a daily schedule for meals, yoga and meditation.
3. This week of "silence" changed my life.
4. When it was time to emerge from the silence, I resisted the chance to talk.
5. There had been a major shift in my awareness and I was experiencing new strong desires for meditation.
6. The day I returned home, I called the Chopra Center in Carlsbad, California, and signed up for the very next class to become a Certified Primordial Sound Meditation Global Instructor.

You, the reader, became part of my synchronous chain of events when you picked up this book. The question now is: Where will meditation take you?

Think of all the inspirations, synchronies, connections, timing, locations and events that have already influenced your life.

These higher levels of consciousness want you to be happy and make choices that create peace, health, love and meaning in your life. Have the synchronies of your life led you to learn about meditation and its powerful effects on the body and mind, to surrender to the wisdom of six thousand years and become a meditator?

Follow your path of events to this moment.

- What was interesting to you about meditation?
- Do you have friends who meditate?
- Did you hear a conversation among meditators?
- Did you meet a teacher with influence? Is it possible that the universe has a plan for you and today is part of that plan?
- Be aware of the moment when you made the decision to accept the new normal of meditation in your life.

Consciousness Connection 2
The Science of Meditation

The serious study of meditation began in 1970, and findings in thousands of published papers, journals and books reveal scientific evidence that a meditative practice produces positive changes in the brain with corresponding physical benefits, among them:

1. Brain wave patterns were far better organized and coordinated.
2. Activity in the brain region associated with positive thoughts and emotions was especially high.
3. Gamma wave activity which is associated with peak concentration, intelligence, IQ, excellent memory and strong self-control increased.
4. EEG and physiological parameters show reduced anxiety and depression and a higher overall sense of well-being.
5. Consistent meditation improves personal performance, reduces drug abuse, the use of prescription drugs and sleeping pills.
6. Meditation improves neuronal interconnections, increases brain tissue volume and increases telomerase activity, which lengthens your lifespan.
7. Reduces age-related memory loss.

Scientists are attending meditation retreats in order to improve their cognitive and emotional skills.

Meditation reduces stress and anxiety, improves relationships, creates inner peace, strengthens intuition, improves sleep, lowers blood pressure, stops over-reactions, improves decision-making, increases executive functions, increases learning ability and levels of intelligence, calms and balances body and mind and enhances immune system function. Meditation is the single most powerful direct means to connect with the mind's deepest level.

Lifestyle changes credited to meditation:

- Better self-care of the body, regular exercise, better choices concerning food, smoking, drugs, alcohol, overeating and other addictions.
- Meditation can change the frequency of the collective consciousness.
- Children who meditate in school have better focus and communication skills, eliminating their overreaction and bullying; it is difficult to fight with someone you have just meditated with.

The overriding question is, with all this proven scientific research, why would anyone not want to meditate?

Consciousness Connection 3
OM Symbol

OM is the primordial cosmic hum in the universe celebrating life and creation. The symbol for OM has 3 curves, a semi-circle and a dot. Together, these elements represent each particle of existence impregnated with energy and consciousness.

1. **Curve #1: Waking State of Consciousness**. The lowest (largest) curve represents your state most of the time, the waking state of consciousness.
2. **Curve #2: Deep Sleep State of Consciousness:** The upper curve represents the unconscious state, that of deep sleep.
3. **Curve #3: Dream State of Consciousness**. The back middle curve is the dream state and it sits between waking and deep sleep.
4. **Dot: The Fourth State of Consciousness.** Called Turiya or Glimpsing the Soul, or Transcendental Consciousness, the Absolute State.
5. **Semi-circle under the dot:** Represents "Maya," the veil of illusion that separates the absolute from the other three curves.

More About the OM Symbol

- **Curve #1: Waking State.** You are awake, working, paying bills, raising a family; you are aware of everything outside of your body. The curve is turned outward to represent your experience of the world through the five senses.
- **Curve #2: Deep Sleep State.** Although you would wake up if a door slammed, there is very little awareness in this state. The subconscious shuts down, desiring nothing and having no dreams.
- **Curve #3: Dream State.** Here, the consciousness is focused inward and you experience a world behind closed eyes; a different view of the universe inside of you.
- **Dot: The Fourth State.** This state transcends; it goes beyond space and time where everything is inseparably connected and synchronized instantly with everything else. This blissful, quiet, peaceful state is the ultimate aim for the spiritual quest.
- **Semi-circle under the dot:** It does not touch the dot, signifying that the Higher States of Consciousness are unaffected by Maya or illusion. It is left open at the top to represent reaching for those Higher States of Consciousness.

Consciousness Connection 4
Chanting OM
The Sound with No Meaning

According to ancient Vedic teachings, the first sound in the universe was "OM". It is the most beloved sound because its frequency and vibration are creation. The vibration of OM awakens the wisdom within for those who chant the sound and for those who hear the chanting of the sound.

1. Chanting the sound "OM" produces a powerful vibration in your bones and cells that continues long after you have stopped chanting.
2. OM is a primordial sound, meaning that it existed from the very beginning of time, a cosmic vibration.
3. Chanting OM is calming, healing and balancing to brainwave patterns. Muscle and skin temperature increases after 2 or 3 minutes of chanting OM.
4. Chanting OM transports us to higher states of consciousness. Chanting releases anxiety, stress, fear, doubt and pain as you become one with the frequency.
5. OM represents the cosmic prana, the vital life force energy.

More about OM

- OM is often at the beginning of a mantra, for example: OM Namaha.
- The sound frequency is considered to be the song of the universe.
- Meditating on OM is acknowledging the Soul, the perfected spiritual person.
- OM represents the 3 Divine powers: Creation, Preservation, Transformation.
- It also represents the 3 Essences of Spirit: Immortality, Omniscience, Joy.
- The OM and AUM sounds are complementary.
- AUM represents the fullness of creation.

Chanting OM

- Begin by feeling the vibration on your lips as you elongate the OM sound (pron. "Ohm").
- As you continue chanting OM, feel the vibration in your belly travel up to the throat and then all the way to the crown of your head.

Consciousness Connection 5
OM and Earth's Rotation

The sound wave frequency of OM is exactly the same as earth's rotation around her own axis – 136.1 Hz. OM is a primordial sound, the sound of the universe at creation; it is the cosmic octave tone of C#.

1. The ever present OM is the pulse of the universe and the source of our whole being.
2. OM is more than a sound, it is the frequency of energy that connects and joins things together.
3. When you open yourself to the vibration of OM you feel yourself grounded to the earth, the cosmos that surround you, and the universe that is inside of you.
4. OM is the eternal sound: the sound of the universe all the time.

Walking in Nature Meditation

- Turn off your phone, if possible.
- Set your intention; tell your mind to become aware and mindful only of this moment.
- Breathe in fresh air and feel it enter and exit your lungs.
- Stop and smell the flowers, take off your shoes and feel the earth between your toes.
- Listen for birds or wildlife, notice the air temperature or breeze.
- Be present with the earth as she is spinning around on her axis.
- Chant OM three times in awareness of your connection with the earth, the cosmos and the universe within you.

Consciousness Connection 6
Mantra, Sound, Energy, Frequency, Vibration

A word has meaning. A mantra is a repetitive sound without meaning which can be thought, heard or chanted to access the higher conscious mind and adjust the vibration of all aspects of your being. A higher or ideal state of being is the ultimate goal of all spiritual disciplines, including the mantra practice.

1. There are thousands of mantras for a variety of purposes, from weight loss or gain, to addressing every type of illness.
2. The vowel sound frequency in each mantra vibrates in the bones, muscles and the fluid tides within the body; it creates a unique vibration in the skull.
3. It is not so much what you hear as it is the biological harmony, frequency and vibration in different body locations.
4. Elongation of the vowel sound provides remarkable healing to the brain and body.
5. Brainwaves begin to balance after three or four minutes and muscle and skin temperature increases.
6. Chanting creates brain chemicals that help neurons communicate with each other, influencing learning and memory.

Experience a Mantra

- Place your hands on your cheeks as you chant, feel the vibrations on your lips and facial bones.
- Each vowel vibrates a different place in your body.
- Chant: ***OM Mani Padme Hum.***
- This mantra is a spiritual sound formula.
- The literal meaning is: Jewel in the Lotus. The sound and frequency invoke compassion.
- It is known as the Prayer of Compassion.
- It is believed to be a vehicle for great personal transformation where anything is possible.

Energy, frequency and vibrations of sounds:

- **OM:** universality and unity, helps us be calm and overcome obstacles.
- **Mani:** mind (the jewel), promotes pure ethics, tolerance and patience.
- **Padme**: unfolding of knowledge and power in the physical chakras and opening of the heart; helps achieve perfection in perseverance and concentration.
- **Hum:** practice of wisdom and purity, integration between heart and mind.

Consciousness Connection 7
Primordial Sound Meditation Mantra

There is even a mantra linked to the exact moment of your birth which can enhance your own personal meditation practice. It is called a Primordial Sound Meditation Mantra.

1. This individual mantra is from ancient Vedic texts and traditions and has been tested for thousands of years.
2. It comes from a mathematical formula based on the position of the Moon and other factors at the time of your first breath of air.
3. This personalized mantra is the sound frequency in the universe at the exact moment of your birth.
4. Knowing your own sound is empowering.
5. There are a total of 108 mantras; one of them is your birth mantra.

Primordial Sound Meditation Mantra

This mantra is unique to the moment of your birth and consists of three sounds chanted in this order:

OM (Birth mantra) Namaha

- *Namaha* represents the frequency of the self, curving back into itself.
- Experiencing your birth mantra, knowing your frequency connection to the cosmos is blissful awareness.
- This mantra connects you to your true, primordial nature.

More thoughts on meditation

- Knowledge is different in different states of consciousness; reality is different in different states of consciousness.
- Enlightenment is the goal of the meditator to experience states of higher consciousness.
- During meditation, we sometimes enter into what is called the gap, when there is no awareness of mantra, thought, time, space or breath. It is the sacred space between our thoughts and our words. The gap is the realm beyond space and time. We do not know when we are in the gap, but suddenly we take a gulp of air as we come out of the gap.

Consciousness Connection 8
How to Meditate

The cell membrane of all fifty trillion cells in your body is a vast communication center and they are all vibrating at the same time and are responsive to every aspect of your life.

1. Your cells are intelligent and are affected by your every thought.
2. Ideally, meditate thirty minutes twice a day.
3. Before breakfast and before dinner is suggested.
4. Or, meditate daily whenever you can.
5. Even five minutes twice a day has a cumulative value for both mind and body.
6. Intention and consistency are key for meditators.
7. Let go of the outcome.
8. Expect nothing.
9. Allow meditation to be whatever it is at the moment.

OM Chant Meditation

- Set the intention: this is my sacred journey.
- Keep it simple, easy and comfortable.
- Turn off the phone if possible; perhaps set a soft, gentle timer.
- Sit upright, close your eyes and allow your body to settle in and just breathe.
- Slowly chant the sound: OM (pron. "Ohm").
- Elongate the "OM" sound.
- Feel your lips and cheeks vibrate.
- Imagine activity in every cell and every bone; your entire being is vibrating.
- Remind yourself that the vibration in the cells will continue long after you have stopped chanting.
- Acknowledge thoughts that come to you and release them, bringing your awareness back to chanting OM.
- Notice the silent space between the OM sound and your thoughts.
- When you have a sense of completion or hear the soft chime of the timer, stop chanting OM and give yourself a couple of minutes to slowly come out of meditation.
- In deep meditation, if you come out of it too quickly or to a loud jarring noise, it disturbs the nervous system.

Consciousness Connection 9
Chakras
Junction Points between Consciousness and the Body

The Sanskrit word *Chakra* translates to swirling wheel or disk of energy. It receives, transforms and distributes the universal life force, energy and information. The human body and the earth body each have seven major chakras.

1. The color spectrum of light affects every living cell and a different color corresponds to each chakra.
2. Each human chakra has a harmonizing musical note, a mantra and a color.
3. Like humans, earth has a physical body and an energetic body.
4. The Earth chakra systems are located **Root** – Mount Shasta, California USA; **Sacral** – Lake Titicaca, Peru-Bolivia, South America; **Solar Plexus** – Uluru-Kata Tjuta, Australia; **Heart** – Glastonbury and Shaftesbury, England; **Throat** – The Great Pyramid, Mount Sinai, and Mount of Olives, Middle East; **Third Eye** – (mobile) western Europe; **Crown** – Mount Kailas, Tibet.

Human Chakra System

- **(8) Soul Star:** Seat of the soul, white & gold in color, located 6 inches higher than the Crown Chakra. When activated, it goes beyond the human ego and fully connects the soul and body to universal enlightenment.
- **(7) Crown**: Located on the top of the head; pure cosmic energy; color – violet.
- **(6) Third Eye**: Centered between the eyebrows; in-sight or blocked by illusion; color – indigo.
- **(5) Throat:** Located in the throat region; truth or blocked by untruth; color – blue.
- **(4) Heart:** Located at the center of the chest; the heart acts as the bridge between the physical chakra and spiritual experiences in chakras five, six and seven; love and compassion or blocked by hatred; color – green.
- **(3) Solar Plexus**: Located at the stomach, two inches above the navel; willpower or blocked by shame; color – yellow.
- **(2) Sacral:** Located at the lower abdomen, spleen area; pleasure or blocked by guilt; color – orange.
- **(1) Root:** Located at the base of the spine in the coccygeal region; survival or blocked by fear; color – red.

Consciousness Connection 10
The Lotus Flower
Symbol of Life's Adversities & Triumphs

The lotus flower is a prevailing symbol of the meditation process and its benefits. It begins its journey as a seed rooted in dark slimy mud. The lotus rises through the water to break the surface and the flower opens to the Sun with no stain or mud on its petals. At night, the lotus closes.

1. The lotus is found in Sanskrit and Tibetan painting. The base of their many statues is the open lotus flower.
2. The lotus is an aquatic perennial. Under favorable circumstances, its seed can remain viable with the oldest recorded lotus germination from seeds 1,300 years old.
3. In Egyptian Mythology, the lotus is associated with the Sun because it blooms in the day and closes at night. The lotus is even believed to have given birth to the Sun.
4. The bud symbolizes potential.
5. The term "jewel in the lotus" represents the mind and enlightenment.

Without Mud There Would be No Lotus

- A closed lotus represents the state before enlightenment.
- An open lotus represents full enlightenment and self-awareness.
- The blue lotus is symbolic of the spirit's conquest of the senses.
- The red lotus represents the compassionate one.
- The pink lotus stands for perfection and is always associated with Buddha.
- The white lotus symbolizes purity of mind and the evolved spirit.
- The purple lotus represents spirituality and mysticism.

The lotus petal count for each chakra is related to certain specific groupings of vertebrae, nerve pairs in the nervous system and spinal column. The petal count of each chakra is:

- Soul Star: eight-petal lotus symbolizes cosmic harmony
- Crown: 1,000-petal lotus symbolizes spiritual illumination
- Third Eye: 2-petal lotus
- Throat: 16-petal lotus
- Heart: 12-petal lotus
- Solar Plexus: 10-petal lotus
- Sacral: 6-petal lotus
- Root: 4-petal lotus

Consciousness Connection 11
Breathing

The primordial impulse is to inhale the first breath before the umbilical cord is cut, followed by approximately seventeen thousand breaths every day or an average of five hundred million breaths in a lifetime. With the last breath, mental and physical functions stop and the life force cord is cut.

1. Breathing is the only autonomic nervous system function you can fully influence.
2. Pranayama, or awareness breathing, is the ancient yogic knowledge of breath movement that consciously influences physical and mental states.
3. There are many forms of Pranayama.
4. Breathe fast or slow, hold the breath, breathe out of your mouth, left or right nostril or both nostrils.
5. Pranayama can energize the body or help you to relax, and even to focus.
6. Awareness breathing enhances the physical, emotional and spiritual self.
7. Awareness breathing is suggested as part of the meditator's daily routine; used just before meditation it can calm and center the mind as your thoughts are integrating inward, away from outer activity.

The Scientific Benefits of Breath Work

- Releases muscle tension.
- Relaxes the body, releases toxins.
- Increases energy levels.
- Reduces anxiety and depression.
- Stabilizes and lowers blood pressure.
- Decreases irritation or anger, feelings of being overwhelmed or over-stressed.
- Calms the nervous system.
- Clears the mind for clarity of thought.
- Increases serotonin levels and other feel-good chemicals.
- Creates a peaceful mind and spirit.
- Engages full capacity of the lungs.
- Increases oxygen supply to the brain.

A Pranayama Breathing Exercise

- **Nadi Shodhana** – A few minutes before meditation, use this alternate nostril breathing exercise for clearing the channels of circulation.
- With your thumb, close the left nostril, inhale through the right nostril, then close off the right nostril and exhale through the left nostril.
- With your thumb, close the right nostril, inhale through the left nostril, then close off the left nostril and exhale through the right nostril.

Consciousness Connection 12
Mala Beads

The mala is a string of beads used to count the repetitions of prayers, mantras or chants. It helps you to focus your awareness and concentration.

1. The standard mala has one hundred and eight beads with a meru (a Sanskrit word for mountain) secured separately from the rest of the beads.
2. The meru is the storehouse for the energy, frequency, vibrational power that builds as you chant or pray with the beads.
3. The mala increases in spiritual potency with use. For that reason, people choose to carry it with them or wear a mala so that the meru is positioned at the back of the skull, allowing the energy to radiate into the brain. Others prefer to wear the mala so that the meru sits over the heart.
4. Half of a mala is fifty-four beads; coincidentally, the Roman Catholic Rosary is also fifty-four beads in length.

How to Hold the Mala Beads

During meditation practice, touch one bead for each time you chant a mantra, then move on to the next bead and the next until you have touched each of the fifty-four or the one hundred and eight beads.

- Using your right hand, drape the mala over the middle finger, the ring finger, and the little finger with the thumb and index finger free.
- With the index finger extended and the thumb touching the top of the first bead, chant the first mantra on this bead.
- The thumb then pushes the mala away so that the next bead comes to rest on the middle finger with the thumb on top of the bead as you chant, repeating these steps until you reach the meru.
- If you want to continue with your mantra meditation once you reach the meru, you can reverse direction and repeat the process.

Symbolically, the three fingers involved in moving the mala beads are considered to represent the three qualities of nature: positive, negative and neutral. The first finger represents the ego and at no time is it to work with or touch the mala. The thumb represents God or the Divine, which is why it is the only digit that moves the mala.

Consciousness Connection 13
Labyrinths

A labyrinth is a walking path with one direct route to the center. You enter, spend time in the center, then exit following the same direct path. Walking the labyrinth is a mini-pilgrimage in the spiral of Sacred Geometry.

1. A labyrinth is not a maze. A maze is a collection of paths from an entrance to a goal with branches and dead ends.
2. As an alternate to physically walking a labyrinth, you can also use your finger or a pointer as a meditation tool to trace a photo of one in a book, or on paper, helping you to focus and calm the mind.
3. Walking the labyrinth represents the life path in the form of a spiritual and physical journey from birth to death and rebirth.
4. Each silent step is an opportunity for prayer, contemplation and meditation; a chance to consciously unwind the mind in a meditative state from stress and worries.
5. Walking the labyrinth offers you insights, creativity, peace and healing.

More About Labyrinths

- The labyrinth is a vortex of energy, spiraling into the field of all possibilities.
- The collective energies of prayer and meditation are here in this sacred spiral earth walk.
- The labyrinth's center is powerful because people spend more time here in contemplation, prayer and meditation.
- Labyrinths have been used for 4,500 years by many different cultures and mystical religious traditions worldwide.
- Currently, there are labyrinths in use at hospitals, universities, churches, spas and backyards to release old patterned behavior, stuck energy, support spiritual alignment and promote energy shifts of expanded awareness.
- The internet has information on labyrinth locations and directions on how to make your own labyrinth.

Consciousness Connection 14
Questions and Answers

1. **Is meditation a trance?**
   No, in a trance the ability to function voluntarily may be suspended. During meditation, you are in a heightened state of active awareness but your body is relaxed.
2. **How can I benefit from meditation?**
   Briefly, scientific data clearly shows that intelligence, awareness and creativity increase; your nervous system calms, reactions to things that once bothered you now don't, you enjoy better relationships and feel happier.
3. **What if I can only meditate once a day instead of twice a day?**
   The world will continue to spin and you are still meditating. Any meditation is better than no meditation at all. Do the best you can. If you only have five minutes, then meditate for five minutes.
4. **Is meditation evil? Can something bad happen to me?**
   No, meditation is not evil. When you meditate, you are simply getting in touch with yourself on a higher level of consciousness.

More Questions and Answers

- **Do I have to think about stuff that is unpleasant when I meditate in order to change it?**
  No, you are only to chant OM or say or think silently your mantra and allow thoughts to come and go. Eventually the body and mind calm down and you naturally release stress.
- **How often do I have to meditate?**
  If you can, meditate daily for 30 minutes twice a day, preferably in the morning before breakfast, perhaps when you first awaken and then again before dinner.
- **Will meditation affect my sleep?**
  You may find that you have less stress and are more rested. However, meditation does not replace regular sleep.
- **I don't feel well. Can meditation help?**
  Meditation restores balance and harmony in the entire mind and body; it supports your immune system. Every cell is intelligent and is always eavesdropping on your thoughts and intentions.
- **I can't stop my thinking during meditation. Is that normal?**
  Thoughts are part of the process. Even the Dalai Lama said he has thoughts while meditating. Simply acknowledge the thoughts and then go back to your meditation.

Consciousness Connection 15
More Questions and Answers

1. **Noise is distracting for me; any suggestions?**
   There will always be noise: a dog barks or the phone rings. The truth is, you cannot always be in a quiet place. Your intention is more powerful than any noise. You are focused and have the intention to meditate. Chant OM or silently repeat your mantra and allow the noise to be while you go deeper into meditation. Acknowledge the noise for what it is, answer the phone, and then return to your meditation. Release any mental attachment to the noise. It is all about your perceptions of the noise. You can even meditate in the airport, or in a train station.

2. **My body has different reactions during meditation. Sometimes it rocks a little and other times it may twitch or jerk. I have even laughed and once I cried. Do other people have these experiences?**
   Your body knows how to release tension and stress with movement. When meditating, acknowledge the body is doing what is best for it and allow the emotions to flow and release. Continue with your meditation. Many meditators experience the body in motion at one time or another.

Even More Questions and Answers

- **Can I eat when meditating?**
  Eating or drinking during meditation is distracting. It is better to meditate before you eat.
- **Sometimes I feel lightheaded after meditation.**
  Lightheadedness, e.g., 'light,' 'energy,' is also consciousness. You may have gone into the 4th State of Consciousness where the field of all possibilities exists. The transition from silence to activity or action takes a few minutes as you slowly and gently come out of meditation. Returning to activity too quickly can be jarring to the nervous system.
- **Will creative thought come to me during meditation?**
  Most of the time the thoughts that come to you during meditation are lists of things you want to do, like grocery shop. If you do have a strong creative thought, acknowledge it for later and return to your meditation. Or, if it feels really important, stop your meditation, write the thought down and then continue your meditation.
- **Why is it different when I meditate in a group?**
  There is coherence group energy; the combined frequencies of a group create a vortex of energy. You become one mind during meditation as the collective frequencies are enhanced.

You've finished. Before you go…

Tweet/share that you finished this book.

Please star rate this book.

Reviews are solid gold to writers. Please take a few minutes to give us some itty bitty feedback.

ABOUT THE AUTHOR

An avid believer in the power of meditation, Rhona is a graduate of Chopra University, where she qualified as a Global Primordial Sound Meditation Instructor for the Chopra Center for Wellbeing. Rhona is also a certified Guided Imagery Therapist and Medical Hypnosis Instructor.

In addition to holding Primordial Sound Meditation classes, Rhona currently works from six clinics in Orange County, California, offering imagery and hypnosis to patients during their medical procedures, and maintains her private practice in Orange. She also offers free monthly meditations at a local hospital in Newport Beach.

Rhona has been honored with a Humanitarian of the Year award in recognition of her work with trauma victims and first responders for the local Trauma Intervention Program. She is also a sought-after motivational speaker. You can reach her at her website: www.rhonaimagery.com or by email at: Rhonaimagery@aol.com

Where will meditation take you?

If you liked this Amazing Itty Bitty® book you might also enjoy…

- **Your Amazing Itty Bitty® Imagery Book** – Rhona Jordan, C.GIt., C.CHt.
- **Your Amazing Itty Bitty® Interstitial Cystitis (IC) Book** – Rhona Jordan, C.GIt., C.CHt.
- **Your Amazing Itty Bitty® Affirmations Book** – Micaela Passeri

Or many other Itty Bitty® books available online.

www.ingramcontent.com/pod-product-compliance
Lightning Source LLC
Chambersburg PA
CBHW061304040426
42444CB00010B/2516